*MORNING WORSHIP*
*and Other Poems*

# MORNING WORSHIP
## AND OTHER POEMS

## MARK VAN DOREN

Harcourt, Brace and Company, New York

Some of these poems originally appeared in
the following publications: *The Antioch Review,
The Atlantic, The Autobiography of Mark Van Doren,
Chicago Review, Columbia University Forum, Harper's
Magazine, The Kenyon Review, Ladies' Home Journal,
McCall's Magazine, The Meaning of Freedom* (published
by the Freedom Fund, Inc., New York, N. Y.), *The Nation,
The New Hampshire Bar Journal, New Poems by American
Poets #2, Pax, Views, The Virginia Quarterly Review.*
Library of Congress Catalog Card Number: 60-5438
Printed in the United States of America

*TO ROBERT LAX*

# CONTENTS

[ 7 ]

## THE SPEECH DEATH MAKES

## ANYTHING BUT BITTER

EPIGRAMS

# ALL SEASONS

# MORNING WORSHIP

I wake and hear it raining.
Were I dead, what would I give
Lazily to lie here,
Like this, and live?

Or better yet: birdsong,
Brightening and spreading—
How far would I come then
To be at the world's wedding?

Now that I lie, though,
Listening, living,
(Oh, but not forever,
Oh, end arriving)

How shall I praise them:
All the sweet beings
Eternally that outlive
Me and my dying?

Mountains, I mean; wind, water, air;
Grass, and huge trees; clouds, flowers,
And thunder, and night.

Turtles, I mean, and toads; hawks, herons, owls;
Graveyards, and towns, and trout; roads, gardens,
Red berries, and deer.

Lightning, I mean, and eagles; fences; snow;
Sunrise, and ferns; waterfalls, serpents,
Green islands, and sleep.

Horses, I mean; butterflies, whales;
Mosses, and stars; and gravelly
Rivers, and fruit.

Oceans, I mean; black valleys; corn;
Brambles, and cliffs; rock, dirt, dust, ice;
And warnings of flood.

How shall I name them?
And in what order?
Each would be first.
Omission is murder.

Maidens, I mean, and apples; needles; leaves;
Worms, and planets, and clover; whirlwinds; dew;
Bulls; geese—

Stop. Lie still.
You will never be done.
Leave them all there,
Old lover. Live on.

## ALL SEASONS

All months, all days, all hours,
All sister seconds even, oh, all seasons
Beautify the world and bless
The walkers on it.

Some of whom they drown,
And some make die of thirst; they burn, they freeze,
They kill us every minute; yet
We must adore them.

Supposing them gone out:
Time's candles. Then no joy or darkness either.
No bitter, sweet; beginning, end.
Oh, mercy on us.

## GET UP, I SAY

Get up, I say, and see them,
The green streaks of morning:
Long and low, with white gold
Alternating, adorning—

Get up, I say; and sometimes,
Just as they are striking,
Obedient I do—ah, those
Lances, so to my liking,

That reach here so straightly,
Unswerving, swinging,
And pierce me—ah, little birds,
Almost to singing.

## AFTER THE WIND AND RAIN

After the wind and rain
How softly the surviving
Subjects of old Sun
Sing hymns to his great age.

He was December's too.
He was before the Flood.
These were not dreamed of then,
But that same father now

Sends hither, one time more,
Sleepy, the sweet love
They sing, and by their singing
Rebuild beyond the world.

# UNDERSONG

## 1

In wonderment I walk to music pouring
Out of so dark a source it makes no sound:
Not waterfalls, not wind, not eagles soaring
On wings that whistle insult to the ground;
Not insect whine at which the flower rejoices;
Not instruments, not voices;
Not, taciturn, those numbers where they wheel
While the fixed stars, creation's counterpoises,
Sing in deep throats a song of commonweal
More ancient than mankind, than beast or bird
Coeval with the Word:
No, none of these is what I overhear
In wonderment, in walking every day.
A harmony more hidden, as midway
Of the whole world it hums, and yet more near,
More secret in my ear,
Keeps coming to me, coming, and I know
As long as I go forth it shall be so.

## 2

Each day I walk in is made slyly one
By symmetries whose names I never seek.
For if I did, and found them, and were done
With listening, with looking, and could speak
Love's language with the subtlety they do,
It might no more be true.
For it is music's language, meant to please
No mind except its own, and if I too
Attempted it the melody would cease;
As birds do in the forest if a foot
Too suddenly is put
On pathways saved for silence, or for such

Plumed echoes as are proper to the place.
The music is not mine in any case;
I only let it come, by sight, by touch,
As often as by hearing; though the ghost
Of sound is innermost;
And mightiest, as if the great one there
Had burst his heart and scattered it in air.


3

Down it falls, that wild unfigured tune
Which nevertheless reorders all my earth.
I walk, and every acre is bestrewn
With witnesses of morning in slow birth,
And of the sky's contentment that things be
Just as they are to see.
Different were deadly, something sings
In a low voice as of a leafy tree
Preoccupied with shade, and two sure wings
That aim at it to enter by and by
When the half-day shall die,
And perfect sunlight shall hang due above
Like a dark lantern swinging. Something says,
Barely aloud, in less than sentences:
Just as they are, together in their love,
The whirlwind, the dove,
The contraries. Listen. That rough chord:
It is his breathing, it is our overlord.


4

In times of tempest when disorder seems
Order itself, the very rule of motion,
And moaning as they bend, the trees and streams,
In horror at their own perverse devotion
To chaos come alive, strain not to shatter

Form, and the first matter
Of which all possibility was made;
But then the roar increases, and winds batter
Winds above the world as fields are flayed
And savage grasses, blowing, strip the bones
Even of sunk stones;
In times of tumult when the lines should snap
That lead like silk from note to kissing note,
And the sweet song should strangle in the throat,
There it still is, miles above thunderclap,
As audible as when on halcyon days
It mastered the same ways;
Compounded of all tones, including these
Of stricken ground and hideous green seas.


5

And if there be those who would mock me, saying:
Music? None is here save in your head;
Noises, yes, delectable, dismaying,
But not in measure, as if more were said
Than owls and larks will tell you, or mad crows,
Or the wind-ravished rose,
Or human chatter, changeless year by year;
Then soberly I say to such as those:
The sound is one, and is not sinister.
It is an honest music through and through.
And so the chatter, too,
And so the silences that wait sometimes
Like a tired giant thinking, so they all
Return and go, then come again and fall,
Evenly, unevenly, as rhymes
Rival the pure chimes
Of never-ending truth, that for so long
Has sung to such as me this undersong.

# DUNCE SONGS

**1**

Where is the bell, the horn,
I hear as I go by,
Go by the invisible wall
That holds up half the sky,
The sky whose other half
Falls down like gold wheat chaff
And sprinkles all the air,
And powders my dull hair?
So people cry and cry:
Who wears that glittery crown,
That crown? And I say I.
Oh, what a falling down
As I go by, go by.

2
If rain rose,
And leaves fell upward—
Oh, me, oh, them
Sky-high together.

That is my house.
Here I am homesick.
Bright, oh, bright,
Forever, ever.

Raindrops, leaves
Round me like mica.
Snow whirls
In a ball of water.

Give it a shake.
That's me in the middle.
White, oh, white—
See now? I am laughing.

3

Some day,
When the great clock
Of dawn strikes, and keeps on striking—
What's gone wrong, the president will shout, why doesn't somebody,
Somebody stop it?—

That day,
When the music starts
That no man ever heard before—
Bong, bong, the bells up there, whish, whish,
The windy singing—

That time
Will be my time:
No minutes, years, no coming, going—
Night, poor night, laid out in white—oh, my soul,
The death of darkness—

Whee, whee,
The waking birds.
(Yet I do pity them a little—
Come close, I'm whispering—yes, I too will miss their brave
Songs at sunset.)

4
Then I'll be four-footed,
And modest with fur.
All over, all under,
Seemly and still.

Then I'll be patient:
A part of the ground.
I will go slowly,
And lowly—oh, sweet,

Then I'll be one of them
He that made all
Looks after the longest,
And tenderest loves.

Then I'll be quiet—
You can be quick—
And lie down all summer,
All winter, and sleep.

5
I have no enemy.
If I did,
I would wait for him, in the black dark, and thwack him—
Ha! on the head.

Or else I would grow
A green worm in my heart
And feed it all day till the strength of its poison
Was death to the world.

Yes, but I have none.
All are my lovers
Harry, and Jack, and even the great ones,
That cause the long wars,

All are my little
Sweet friends that I wait for,
In the warm sun, and stroke them, stroke them—
Ha, my poor head!

6

Her hand in my hand,
Soft as the south wind,
Soft as a colt's nose,
Soft as forgetting;

Her cheek to my cheek,
Red as the cranberry,
Red as a mitten,
Red as remembering—

Here we go round like raindrops,
Raindrops,
Here we go round
So snug together,

Oh, but I wonder,
Oh, but I know,
Who comforts like raisins,
Who kisses like snow.

7

If I had a wife
I would love her as kings
Loved queens in the old days, or as princes
Maidens,
Met in the dew, by a stile, of a morning—
"How do you do, my pretty?"
And all of that.

If I had a wife
I would come home sometimes
Dressed like a stranger, and when she stared,
"Lady,"
I'd say, and woo her in wonder—
"How can there be such shining?"
And all of that.

If I had a wife
I would never be done
With remembering how it is now when, oh,
I am lonesome,
And no one is here but my dog and my cat—
"Well, old boys! Hungry?"
And all of that.

## 8

Pepper and salt
And summer savory—
Those are for luckier tables and tongues
Than my old woman
And I have.

The sun and the wind,
Those are our seasoning;
With maybe nine drops of rain on a Thursday—
Yes, my old woman's
A smart one.

She holds up her bonnet
Just when He is looking—
Oh, the love in His eyes, oh, the millions of tears.
Even my old woman
Is weeping.

9

Love me little, love me long,
Then we neither can be wrong:
You in giving, I in taking;
There is not a heart breaking
But remembers one touch,
Or maybe seven, of too much.

Love me more than halfway, though.
Let me think, then let me know.
And I promise you the same:
A little wild, a little tame;
Lest it ever seem long:
Tick, tock, ding, dong.

# LOVERS MUST WONDER

# THE LOVE SONGS OF OBERON

*Proem*

Titania is queen
Of fairyland and me;
But woman first of all,
And mistress, and girl.
Listen to me then.
I am as other men.

## Titania's Eyes

There are no eyes as black as night
Except Titania's by the sea;
Or in the forest, or this room—
Oh, anywhere they look at me
They burn the rest of darkness out
As absolute consumes degree.

More black than black, Titania's eyes,
As if a candle dimmed the sun;
As if a tear outwet the waves,
Or certain stars resisted dawn.
Blazing black, Titania's eyes;
And I am the consumèd one.

For in the darkness of this room,
And in my own dark where I lie,
Remembering ocean or the woods,
With sweet Titania standing by,
Suddenly, more near than near,
She darkens darkness, and I die.

*My Love Comes Walking*

My love comes walking,
And these flowers
That never saw her till this day
Look up; but then
Bend down straightway.

My love sees nothing
Here but me,
Who never trembled thus before;
And glances down
Lest I do more.

My love is laughing;
Those wild things
Were never tame until I too,
Down-dropping, kissed
Her silvery shoe.

*Lute Song*

So soft her voice, so drooped her head,
I did not then suspect the power
She had to be rememberèd.

For nothing dies of that first hour
When there she walked, and all her gaze
Flowed down as to a sister flower.

Not then to me, nor through these days
That wander since and hold their breath:
Never to me, who yet do praise

This strength in her, more strict than death,
That where I go it followeth,
That where I go it followeth.

## How Can It Be?

She is woman, she is wife,
Yet is a maiden to the life:
Mine, or yours, or anyone's
Who shall be first and rudest—runs
And throws her down among the flowers,
Aha! as sudden thunder showers
Can blast a blossom. There she lies,
Half-buried, weeping; yet will rise
And be as ignorant again
As if there were no husbandmen.
God of storms, how can it be
That nothing wracks her? Who are we,
That she survives us? What am I,
Who will not live to see her die
When all the world ends—oh, the woe
Of springtime that must watch her go!

*Slowly, Slowly*

The lover loves the eyes that close,
And closing, shut the world to shame;
Then parted lips; then helpless blood;
Then breast and breast, the two, the same,
The all in one, awaiting there
Himself, the other—hears his name—

And answers; but he loves the most
What now he neither hears nor sees,
Yet has at last—oh, wonder then—
Down there—his very own—the knees
That slowly, slowly melt his bones
As summer sun drowns honey bees.

## Dressed, Undressed

Dressed, undressed: the difference leaps
Millenniums, past even time
Millenniums, for where it lands
Is then, is there, is everywhere,
Oh, dizziness, is everywhen,
Is furlongs east of Eden, miles
From nowhere if nowhere is now,
Is now, is all this blushing blood,
This blinding modesty made free
Of there, of then, of self and shame
And nowhen. Now, oh, only now,
And here, oh, only here, take off,
Take off, Titania, everything,
Take off the least thing that can cling,
The least, the last thing—there, oh, there,
Titania—nothing, nothing left
But you, but me, in one lone world
Of millions that were here till now,
Till now, Titania, now, till now.

## *This Way, That Way*

Titania, be still
And let me love you as I will;
This way, that way—yes, and more:
To ten;
But then,
Why not a score?

Titania, look up
And let me; nightlong now look up
And let me, and keep softest count;
Till number
Slumber,
And day mount.

Titania, sleep there
And let me lie as light as air
At last upon you; till the sun,
Our friend,
Descend,
And you say one.

Titania, say two,
And love whatever I shall do
Until the darkest of our days;
Till light
Be night
Always, always.

# THE LOVE SONGS OF OBERON

*Love to Come*

Titania is weary,
Not with love over, but with love to come,
My love, her love, one love together,
Drowning as in a dream, but that's to come,
Titania, expectant of this honey hour,
Deliciously—I see it—is love weary.

Her eyelids tell me,
And the slow way, as if in heavy water,
Indifferent to deepest death,
She comes where I am, comes, and passes me,
Drowning as in a dream, but I can reach
And save her, die with her one death together.

Titania knows well
How weariness bewitches me, her lover—
Similitudes of sleep,
How all of them become her in this honey
Hour when nothing more of love seems possible,
Then is, then is, and so we dream we drown.

*Titania's Own Love Song*

Day, be long aborning.
Stir not in the womb.
Let this one night be childless—
O, sweet bridegroom,
O, lover dark by me,
Whisper: do you agree?

Your hyacinth loves sun;
My columbine weeps tears
Lest morrow never wake.
It must. But oh, the years,
Sweet lover, we shall spend
Before evening's end.

Night, be no mother now
Bring forth no bird nor flower;
Be mistress of old Time
With whom he wastes an hour.
My king is young—yet see,
Ah, how we agree.

# LOVERS MUST WONDER

These little birds that feed all day so fiercely,
All week, all winter, keeping their hearts hot—
Gems in feathers—why such a length of labor?
Is it for love in June, or have they forgot?
Was something less intended by their maker:
That they maintain mere fire? Oh, no? Then what?

When mistresses all morning move in coolness,
Speaking and doing: daughters of mankind;
Was it for this the mother of their being
Put, without difference, tongue in them and mind?
Lovers must wonder. How does such clear seeing
Measure night's minutes, animal, blood-blind?

# LOVE LIVES ON

Child-bearing Bess, bedraggled proof
That love lives on in this poor world,
Is no temptation; she can pass,
And no man dreams of her as curled—
Golden caterpillar—on his bed,
With crushed white pillows about her head.

Yet love lives on; she is the sign,
And one man sees it. Where is he?
In what damp corner does he wait—
Earth's worm—till both again shall be
All that they were when Bess went by
And he was bedazzled as by sky?

So long had he withheld his hands,
She found him slow to learn:
The way a breast, a thigh, can yield;
The way snow can burn.

You thought me once a goddess, boy,
And so I am, she said;
Desire like this is not of earth:
More, and we both were dead.

Oh, no, he cried; but even then,
Like one brand ablaze,
They broke and fell, and each went out
As stars extinguish days.

# I HAVE COME HOME AGAIN

I have come home again;
Not from so very far;
But love computes absence
As, star beyond star,
Worlds turn to nothing,
And chaos is there.

I have come home again;
Not since so very long;
But love measures meetings
As, song beyond song,
Joy turns to brooding,
And hushes its tongue.

Lady, excellently brief
(Let me be too),
The sweet things you say
Are salt also,
For true.

It takes my very breath, the mixing,
As if I tried
To be both hot and cold
Together; lived,
And died.

As if within a summer sky
Some lightning hid;
Not to be found except
As on love's day
You did.

# COMPLIMENT

Comparing her with gold,
Deriving her from queens,
I look for such a smile
As measures those extremes;

And seeing it, reply
With such a thankful grin
As testifies we know,
Both of us, the mean;

For which no word exists;
It is ideal and dark:
The lodestone, down there,
That keeps our love at work.

# IF YOU BUT DREAMED IT

God's love does not compute desert
In birds and worms, in bones and dirt.
He kisses all things where they lie;
And if they run, or if they fly,
The very air they antic through
Is theirs till death, which he gives too.

Can you love me as He loves these
Great stones and bones and starting trees?
You never made me—yes, I know;
But you can slay me, quick or slow,
By not beginning, my sweet friend,
To own me without thought of end,

As He does, He does. Listen now
To that small warbler on the bough.
He lets him sit, He lets him sing,
As if he were the chiefest thing.
And so he is; and so am I
If you but dreamed it, standing by.

## LITTLE TRIP

Let's go. Let's be somewhere awhile
We haven't ever been before;
And strangers cut the random grass
Or leave it ragged. That can pass;
For now the road climbs more and more,
And we are silent mile by mile
Between whose woods? We'll never know
Unless we stop to read his name.
Up and over, down and on
Around this mountain, blue then brown.
Here is a river, wild or tame
According as the rocks below
Be few or many. Next a house,
And neat or not we like it well,
For someone else does all the chores
Or doesn't do them. Churches, stores—
There, I heard the crossing bell.
So home by dark to moth and mouse.

# I AM NOT EVER

The desert moor, the empty glen:
I am not ever, travelling by your side, so much at home
As then.

The swept road, the swift car,
Flying, flying on the wings of those forsaken worlds,
As far

As God's body, death's end:
I am not ever, dear, so deep in love with you; nor you
With wind.

## SECOND THOUGHT

I have not waited to praise this woman.
Some day it will be forty years since I began.
But a tale now, and a song then—could I have believed
Stuttering like that became a man?

Well, then, the full word. I say it loud at last. . . .
What do you mean, you heard nothing?
Why, it was one wave, gathering back yonder,
That came all the way unbroken; then burst.

But I see now. It did not break. It keeps going,
Through me and on. Over, too, and back under:
One with the deep world, the dark and round.
Well, then, no praise. No insult of sound.

TO THE AUTHOR OF *Hesperides*
AND *Noble Numbers*

Herrick, hello.
You cannot be asleep; and yet if so,
Kinsman, your book is not: the lyric
Spring, unquenchable, of him I know,
Robert, as my Herrick.

And I am his,
And therefore yours, like those nine mistresses
Who never spoke one word, yet wore
The crimson ribands and the stomachers
You still I think adore.

I do but read,
Herrick, I do but listen; yet indeed
All that you asked was eyes and ears.
Well, mine are thine, and I shall intercede
With others to give theirs.

Herrick, be sure
Your maids, your meadows, and your verse endure,
And your delicious lewdness, drawn
By the same sun, that loves impure with pure,
From him I dote upon.

If we had mistresses, my old
Deep-sleeping friend—if you and I,
That once outwatched the flowery cold
And saw each brilliant planet die
Love's death at summer daybreak—now,
In winter, if we did somehow

Have pretty mistresses, my friend,
And I should name them, would you hear?
You can but feel, yet in the end
You knew those others: hot and clear
By heart you had them, so that I learned
Only from you how fierce we burned,

Yourself and me—oh, that young night,
And oh, now this decrepit day.
For I shall keep the secret tight
Of these green girls with whom I stray,
Unknown to you, unguessed by them,
Devouring blossom, bud, and stem

Till each is in me like a cool
Life-giving herb; for I confess
There is no rage in my misrule;
My lust is leaf, is marrowless.
And that is all; so sleep again
Under our snow, ancient of men.

# THE SPEECH DEATH MAKES

# TIME WAS WHEN DEATH

Time was when death
Seemed mountain, or myth;
Alien to world;
Green oceans away.

Time was when the end
Seemed a pouring of sand;
And the last fine grain—
That glittered the most.

Time was; time is;
And this morning death says:
Stand there; I am here;
I am all that will be.

His language is plain:
Very like to my own.
But the one dark word
Is the sound of my name.

Time still is to be
When I am not I.
The speech death makes
Is not special for me.

# LITTLE MY SOUL

Little my soul,
How long will you live?
And where, if not here?
And why, if I die?

Little my life,
Who had you before?
And who will be next?
And again? What then?

Little my breath,
Did you never stop?
Were you never so cold
That known was unknown?

Little my soul,
You and I are the same;
Are warm, and are one.
Peace be till we cease.

Stronger than minds of men—
Almost than His, than His—
Strange, but the learner learns
Only what is, what is.

Learns to lie down one day;
Suffers himself to be bound;
So then the turning, turning,
Cold and slow, around.

Yet after years a pressure,
As of contraction's heat,
Sometimes to the pure center.
There is no name for that.

Nor any name for the turning,
Spread-eagled, upon a sphere
He will be learning, learning
Until light disappear.

## OLDEST CEMETERY

I go downhill some days to a little room
Where the first people put their souls to sleep,
And where four walls of fallen fieldstone keep
Close rumor of their names, with verses cut
(I lie and read) against forgetful doom.
Remembered, they would rise in fields of rest
As far away as east is from the west;
Or farther, past all compass; for they shut
This wilderness of time, of nature out;
They thought to wake in such a world of light
As no man works for, warned of coming night;
Pure joy and peace it was. And so they put
Each weary soul to bed, with owls and crows
To watch, and weeds to deepen its repose.

Some days I think the end has come and gone.
Sound fell, and they got up, and where they lay
Was nothing now but litter as away
On wings they went and had their dream at last:
The universe was over. Time goes on
As always, and the same birds in the sky
Declare it, but without hope's reason why:
Tick, tick, until the finish. Or, no blast
Of horns was heard, no host of angels passed;
It all was childish error, and these stones
But tilt above time's waste. And whose the bones?
The verses tell. I ponder them, steadfast,
Expectant. No, the end is coming still
For such as these, on this forgotten hill.

The small minds of birds,
Perfect in the wind or on the bough;
The sleek thoughts of those that go on four feet,
Eyes wide, without a mark left by their looking—
The same world is there,
Dozing in honey air—

Men do not leave things so.
Their dreaming hardens into chimneys, towers,
Walls, chambers for the living, for the dead—
Hopefully, forever; though these objects
Rot. Yet are replaced.
Idea is not erased.

Could it be spider fine,
Or finer: even no thin silk to blow;
Could a man's brain not monument itself,
Not litter that sweet sleep—O tell him, You
That made man more than beast,
How like most is to least.

# THE SACRIFICE

As soon kill God as kill one of His creatures.
He wrote this dying, and the doves around
Flew off in fear because the paper fluttered.
They did not know he starved on stony ground;
They did not know he saved them out of love
For every breath beneath him or above.

And though his own was lost, he loved it too,
And wondered at the end if he did well.
But there was not a sign of Yes or No;
Not a stone rose, nor softest feather fell
To say which sacrifice had been preferred
By Him who made them equal, man and bird.

If equal truly. So this man believed,
And so he proved he did, in the extreme;
But only after dark knew God's desire,
That may have been blood brother to his dream
Of such a love twixt intellect and beast
As spares those most who comprehend it least.

# THE LAUGHING PHILOSOPHER

The laughing philosopher sits on his tomb
With an old friend, a lover of cypresses,
And drinks all afternoon to lovely death;
"Who may not come tonight," he sips and says,
"But come she will; she is the only lady,
Living or no, that keeps her promises."

"Lady? Alive?" And now the friend is laughing.
He is himself a cypress, bald and green.
"If lady, why not lipless?" And he grins.
But the philosopher, as to his queen,
Lifts high another cup. "I think she lives.
I grant you, though, she never has been seen."

"Then why say she? You are too obstinate.
Death could be animal; be wind, or worm;
Be anything; be nothing." "Nothing? No.
Death is my lady, and her lips are warm
For speech and then for kissing." "O, lovesick
Philosopher!" "Aha! And what the harm?"

# AND SO IT WAS

And so it was
That Achilles, wounded of mind, called to his beautiful mother.
His honor had been hurt, and she must heal it.
She did; but opened a deeper wound, the death of Patroclus;
Whence rivers of blood in which all Troy was drowned.

And so it was
That Odysseus, grizzled darling of Pallas Athene,
Triumphed over the waves; then on dry land,
His enemies. But the grey waves, still reaching, rocked him
Nightly, and robbed the old fox of his rest.

And so it was
That Hamlet, friend of angels, was elected by the fiend
To weed the bed of Denmark, and plucked up,
Before he knew it, flowers; till all was waste
And woe, and the prince of roses died himself by prick of thorn.

And so it was
That once in poor La Mancha thought grew rich,
Put forth, and filled the world; which, being full
Already, groaned aloud, fearful of surplus; and the vine,
Weary of its own leaves at last, withdrew.

And so it was
And is, and will be ever: no good man but finds the going
Strange; and yet he goes; and we that watch him
Wish we too had gone where wolf and worm,
Surprising a brave soul, work out their wonders.

## IN ATHENS, THOUGH

In little Greece, great mountains:
Walls of an old world that only eagles and the ghosts
Of heroes (Agamemnon in his shroud)
Remember, and that only
Women such as walk there now can wear
Like sadness on their shoulders, in their eyes.
Their smile assumes sobriety
In strangers too; the wind
Is one to them and these; the hard,
High, marvellous brown mountains are a wingèd
Weight they share with who comes up,
Comes down the stony passes, and is nightly
Glad for olives, ancient on the plain.

In Athens, though, a honey-sweet
Old wrinkled woman, captive of the suburbs,
Beamed when her son said "Delphi";
Beamed, holding my hand in hers, and said it after him
As a girl says a lesson; said it softly,
"Delphi, Delphi," twice, for then, for now:
Her birthplace, and her second childhood's
Innermost clandestine pleasure
Hugged here in this faraway new house
Where lights mean other houses, not the stars.
"Delphi." And I saw her halfway up
Parnassus, gathering thyme, the flowery food
Of old ancestor bees long since
In Hades, mourning the hot sun.
I saw her, not in shadow, bearing
Both of those huge tawny summits,
Desolate, for burden, smiling
Ruefully, remembering,
Remembering,
Not here but there,
Not now but then and then,
The cries of heroes (Laius in his car).

They left him hanging for the deed
His black-eyed brother did.
And still beneath that basswood tree
No wildflower goes to bed.

No daisy but is darker there
For staring all night long
At something once the wind turned round,
Careless of right, of wrong.

They came next day and cut him down,
And the false brother groaned.
But still the black-eyed Susans gaze
At what the wind turned round.

And would, if any man could read,
Tell what was done amiss.
But no man now remembers it,
So long ago it is.

# NAP

I lay me down, but down is deep
Past dark, past death, past deep's idea;
Is the soft seas themselves, that drain
Away as my own mind does, my own
Bones that will not be, not be
Again; not be my bones; not my
Own bones, that settle separately,
Softly, down and down—oh, sweet
Non-being, not my own, wherein
I sink like light in water, dimming
Slowly, oh, so slowly, deep
By deep, beyond the dark of death's idea.

# ANYTHING BUT BITTER

Rage in the mildest mind,
A mute world assisting—
Contradictories grown dumb;
The mystery made lasting—
Rage so deep, so pure,
Is not unwise or wasting.

It may be that the glint
Is anything but bitter
Of ardor in those eyes,
Staring out at matter:
The urgency to love
Deity's dead letter.

## THE TIME I WASTED

The time I wasted built the world.
Lazily looking, there it was.
Piecemeal, the frame emerged;
Or most of it; some never has.
And never will; the mind's work,
Proud thing, leaves vacancies.

If I could only waste it all.
But, temporal, nobody can.
If I could only have it whole.
But mortal thought turns always in.
To know itself, the single will
Must mutilate that sizeless one.

# THE WAVES

The waves of air and ocean
And the dark sea of nothing between stars;
Or if not nothing, something; but no matter,
There they go galloping as if in eagle
Wind, in dolphin water; yet not so—
Oh, widest world, oh, nameless,
Nervous,
Nothing if not something: curl on curl
Out, out, and out—sometimes
It causes me to tremble,
Tremble,
Sometimes it causes me down here,
Oh, way down solid here,
To shake and tremble.

The aging heart: is it more filled with kindness,
Having more room—O memory, more room—
Or does a colder person occupy it:
A dusty miller, or a rich bridegroom
Who comes too late for love, and lays him down
With icy gold for maiden and bedgown?

The youthful heart says yes: what age forgives
Is age; at greener folly it but groans;
It finds the children witless whom it else
Might wonder at; their delicate breastbones
It taps and says not tough enough, not steel;
Time aches to eat of it, poor flesh, inchmeal.

Both hearts are bitter when they think thiswise
And not of love alone: which if they do,
Then grief in them is for their own defect;
But joy is for the strength that can renew,
Oh, instantly, the charity they lost
When judge and angel, deep in them, crisscrossed.

## SOME DAY THEN

Old men's intensities are not to be believed.
Their pities and their rages, humorous, unterrible,
Return and burn again, building a whiter ash
About a hotter fire. some day, some day, unbearable.

Some day then it is clear: soul must consume itself.
After so many trials, nothing but ache, but error.
So with no world to watch, and neither with smoke nor flame,
Simply it burns and burns; and no tale of the terror.

# THE TIME TO COME

Two young hearts in five old rooms
But the first ever, being theirs:
Experience, transplanted, blooms
And with good weather wisely bears;
And will be harvested some day;
But that is worlds on worlds away.

Why do I jump the time to come?
It is but starting; will be slow;
Will stop, they think, and hang and hum
Like wind with no good where to go.
Yet in that sweetness let them be.
Time may stand still. It raced with me.

## PARENTS' RECOMPENSE

Those that we hovered,
Holding our breath,
Suddenly see him,
Granduncle Death,
Walking close by.
So we are to die.

Not yet. We are strong.
But it is their turn
To indicate love
By excess of concern.
They do; and we smile
All the last mile.

## YOUNG HERBERT

Young Herbert on his hill and I on mine
Do not forget each other. What he thinks,
I wonder. But he thinks. I know by how
He takes so long a look when we descend
And meet. And maybe smile. If we do not,
The choice was his. The younger and the stronger
Quietly decides. Immense and fair,
He rules me. When he waves I am as glad
As if a wild god noticed. When we speak,
The best I do is listen. Once he called
Me captain, and saluted my great age.
He may believe me dying: what if that,
And only that? If so, I do not tell him
Both of us are doomed. For all I know,
He isn't; generations of old men
May go downhill each morning as I do
And wait for him and gamble that he smiles.

# THE CHILD AT WINTER SUNSET

The child at winter sunset,
Holding her breath in adoration of the peacock's tail
That spread its red—ah, higher and higher—
Wept suddenly. "It's going!"

The great fan folded;
Shortened; and at last no longer fought the cold, the dark.
And she on the lawn, comfortless by her father,
Shivered, shivered. "It's gone!"

"Yes, this time. But wait,
Darling. There will be other nights—some of them even better."
"Oh, no. It died." He laughed. But she did not.
It was her first glory.

Laid away now in its terrible
Lead coffin, it was the first brightness she had ever
Mourned. "Oh, no, it's dead." And he her father
Mourned too, for more to come.

# WISH FOR THE WORLD

Wish for the world that it will never change,
Even if terrible, to total strange.
Even if good, may there be no excess
Beyond this power to think of more, of less,
That is our lone reward for living here.
May only what is missing still be clear
On any earth to come, that so can teach
Hell's difference, and heaven's—each from each,
And both from its dear self: the single place
Than which all others have exacter grace,
And yet it is the measure. Be it thus
Forever, little world that lengthens us.

# THE WORLD IS KIND

# IN BITTERNESS OF HEART

In bitterness of heart I write,
But gentleness of mind;
For thinking slow, I may remember
That the world is kind.

Or was; or would be; and contains,
Like dew within the rose,
Some delicate, some hidden friends.
I must remember those.

And so I do; and drop by drop
I am rewarded well;
By tincture; or as weeping gold
Tempers the harsh bell.

## CARL

Like a great tree
Spread over me,
With love in every limb:
I worshipped him.

# AND STILL THE SAME
*(To Joseph Wood Krutch)*

He differs day by day,
Or else I do.
Yet it is not my way
Thus to be ever new
And still the same:
Both wild and tame;
Both added to and one
When that is done.

It seems no more than chance
That changes him.
And molecules do dance,
I know, and atoms swim.
With this man, though,
It is not so.
Surprising to the end,
He is my friend.

Not that his wit consents.
He hides his heart.
So it is my pretense,
And both of ours the art,
Thus to despise
What never dies;
What never will be done
Till many is one.

## WOE, WOE
*(To Robert Lax)*

Woe, woe. The long face,
Patiently, in hoarse wind,
Meditates, meditates,
Without a word that men hear.

When they do, and I have,
What a seeing, what a song.
Not a thought but thanks God
For bird and leaf and Sunday morning.

Snow, rain: exactly so.
Mountains; or if need be, none.
Men, women: who but these,
The now, the here? And what delight.

Woe, woe. The mournful eyes
Should never have misled us. Listen.
Angel clear and sparrow sweet:
Love, love is all there is.

Good, good: how get it said
In man's time? God is long.
Maybe that: he really mourns.
The night comes. So much unmentioned.

# ONCE IN KENTUCKY

*(To Thomas Merton)*

In our fat times, a monk:
I had not thought to see one;
Nor, even with my own poor lean concerns,
Ever to be one.

No. But in Kentucky,
Midway of sweet hills,
When housewives swept their porches, and March light
Lapped windowsills,

He, once my merry friend,
Came to the stone door,
And the only difference in his smiling was,
It sorrowed more.

No change in him, except
His merriment was graver.
As if he knew now where it started from;
And what the flavor.

He tasted it, the joy,
Then gave it all to me:
As much, I mean, as I could carry home
To this country,

To this country whose laughter
Is a fat thing, and dies.
I step across its body and consider,
Still, those eyes.

# THE WONDER IS
*(To Robert Caldwell)*

Massive the man, massive the wrath;
He girds at public liars, thieves;
Unreason so enrages him
He trembles like a tree, with leaves,
And might come down; except his strength
Is delicate, both breadth and length.

The wonder is at last the soul;
It sits in him, beside his heart,
And sings as if a stranger wound
The key to it and gave it start;
It sings of things that cannot be:
For instance, he delights in me.

In so much bigness, something perfect—
Not that I prove it—something old;
As if his giant maker said,
Let this be in him, small and gold,
To sit each day beside his wrath
And sing like love of truth and death.

# LIKE MICE, LIKE FLOWERS
*(To José Villa)*

Look. The stone face—
It is not stone, but the soul's grace
That he met early (he was not young long),
Frozen.

Look. Now, years away,
See the hot subtleties that play
Like mice, like flowers, like rain, yet never
Melt it.

Look. Sweet mercy's worm,
Within him, still cannot make infirm
His judgment: silver gentle, iron
Decisive.

# ANGER IS, ANGER WAS
*(To James Thurber)*

The tumult in this shouting man
Gives way at once to dove's words.
Anger is, anger was,
But half between is holy ghost
Descending out of time gone.

The memory of this hunted man
Is barking wolves, is fool's gold.
But here a wing, and there a wing,
And all within is sleepy peace.
He walks again the good world.

# PHILOSOPHER AT LARGE
*(To Mortimer Adler)*

The ancient garden where most men
Step daintily, in specimen dust,
He bulldozes; plows deep;
Moves earth; says someone must,
If truth is ever to be found
That so long since went underground.

What truth? Why down? He shakes his head.
He does not know. But roots and rocks
Go tumbling, tearing, as his blade,
Shivering from its own shocks,
Bites farther, and upturns pure clay
He does not pause to smooth away.

And horrifies those men, by hedge
And dust plot, whom the top sufficed.
They thought the garden theirs. And still
It is; but the dead air is spiced
With damp new things dug up. Or old,
He says; like God, like buried gold.

# BETWEEN OUR VOICES
*(To Allen Tate)*

He was the soonest friendly,
But then the soonest tired;
As if between our voices,
Suddenly, a third,
More intimate than either,
Said something thin and weird,

And he must listen closely,
Though not to me or him;
As if the ancient mother
Of every man had come,
And only he might fathom
Her words of sleep, of home,

Of going back to places
Before a thought was had;
As if the world's conception
Still waited, and instead
There was this womb of ocean,
And none but him inside.

# HIS THOUGHTS ARE KISSES
*(To John Tagliabue)*

He walks in a fine fire of atoms
So continual, like light about his head,
That he has never dreamed of cold or storm,
Or nakedness disgusted with itself, or envy
Poisoning used arrows to be shot again,
This time to reach and kill.

He walks in the first mist, the one
Before creation rested. He is affection
Not yet distilled, distinct: incapable of dying.
His thoughts are kisses, fecund as the weightless
Waters of the deep love turned that day to spray;
And still they dance in him.

# MY GREAT FRIENDS

My great friends do not know me.
Hamlet in the halls,
Achilles by the river, and Don Quixote
Feasting with the Duke see no one there
Like me, like Mark Van Doren, who grows daily
Older while they look not, change not,
Die not save the deaths their masters made.

Those, yes, over and over.
And Bottom stands tremendous,
And Sancho rubs his head, half comprehending
Knighthood, and Malvolio's cold voice
Invites the madhouse hour. These neither die
Nor rise again. They look not, change not,
Only as folly, wonderful, lasts on.

Still my great friends ignore me,
Momently grown older
And dying in the west. They will be there
Forever, gods of the world, my own immortals
Who will not go along. Nor do I ask them.
Let them forever look not, change not,
Die not save as mortals may behold.

# THE GOOD OF STILLNESS

# COUNTRY BOREDOM

Whole days are city minutes if you measure
Time by persons. Less. For no one comes.
Ticktock is not a footstep, nor does wind
Wear clothes. Nor does sunset speak to sunrise;
They are not even strangers to each other,
Here in this waste of purpose, in this faceless
Forum where the atoms never argue:
Equal and indivisible; content
With the vast void between them. If you count
By voices, music fails; and if you listen
Only for wit there is no need of ears.
What then? Why stay? What is the good of stillness,
Had at so huge a cost? I will not tell you.
I do not know. Except, with stillness itself
For standard, I could be satisfied, and am.
Listen. No one comes. That wasn't the wind.
Even the clock is holding its breath; and the stars
Have stopped. Or I think they have. Be quiet. Thinking
Itself is sound. We shouldn't be here. Or if so,
We shouldn't be disagreeing. Even agreeing.

# SWEET WILLIAM'S BREATH

Sweet William's breath,
Clove pink, clear spice,
Has breathed upon me twice,
Boy and man:
In my gaunt grandmother's garden,
Then my own—hot, sweet,
Here it is, and candy good;
Here it is, red, white,
And small and many, like the figures
In her apron long ago.
Gaunt she was, and still, and good,
My life ago.

# HIGH AUGUST

More things thrive in the sun
Than my sweet people and me:
The snake; the venomous vine;
The weasel; the wild bee;
And over us all sometimes,
Thunder, suddenly.

The world, put forth this while,
Threatens our breathing room;
Buzzes, and strikes; but then
Winter is soon to come;
We shall be few again,
And loving, and lonesome.

# DEPARTURE: SEPTEMBER

He has driven away, and with him has gone
More even than summer, though that is as much
As I look for this morning; and see on the lawn—
Look, leaves fallen, and dry to the touch.

More than warm green, than lazy long growth,
Went down the cool hill with him only last night.
I am here, he is there: it is each, it is both
Things sicken me now with their secret delight;

As if it were good to devour an old heart;
As if it were pleasure to leave in its place
A dry, small mind whose meagerest art
Will be to remember his hands and his face:

How he did this, and how he said that,
And how he was angry for part of one day;
As if it were better to sit where he sat
Than to have him still here and deciding to stay.

## DANCE OF DEATH

Fall is a crazy dancer—
Look, how he whirls in leaves;
How happy Death is to be stamping with him—
There, on the stricken body
Of grass, of mortal green.

Down with it all: he dances,
And look, she laughs in his arms;
Wicked, the bright wind is funeral music
For long days—remember?—
And hot dark, and flowers.

Death is a wild partner;
But look, she is not young.
She is the eldest daughter; she has danced
Forever, without wedding
Any warm one.

## WITH APPLES

The last leaves are down, and the iron
Trunks, solitary, say they can stand there
Seven cold months without perceptible
Change. But the green ground changes
Daily, so that Hallaway's old horses,
The brown one, the black one,
Nibble at next to nothing where the hoar frost
Of hours ago gave way before the yellow and still blowing,
Blowing—some of them purple—leaves.
These move, head down, but listen:
Someone may be coming, even now, in the bright wind,
With apples. I am coming.
Four pockets full, and extras on the hip.
Hi, there, Handsome Jerry!
Don't you know me, Slobbery Mack?

# THE ANGLE OF THE SUN

The angle of the sun—O, artist,
Summer and winter you dispose these bands
Of shadow with a master ease. They lie,
Dark sleepers, where you let them fall:
So beautiful, so bodiless, so less than black,
So willing to be walked on; or—
Look now—
So perfect in their stroke, so brushed,
Thick, thin, that all the world outside this window
Is one in secret cunning with your amber
Mind, O, artist cool and warm together,
Strict and sweet,
O, painter loved and loving
Of slant lines across a yard.

## SAY WHICH

This afternoon I think I'll pile
The apple wood that David split;
Or rake and sweep the dirt floor
Down cellar; or, if the wind dies,
Assemble the last mountain of this year's
Leaves, and drag it off to rot in rain
And snow while no one notices; or climb
And shut the attic louvers—it is time;
Or stuff the window cracks; or clear
The strainer by the pond; or hang
The tools where they belong; or—oh, my lucky
Stars, the list is endless; I am rich;
I can say which
Of all these good, clear, shapely,
Solitary things
I'll do;
And show to you.

# INCINERATOR

Mornings, in a stone place,
I worship fire the cleanser.
I go there; he meets me;
And one scratch does it all.

The paper, the wet bones;
Last evening's greenstuff:
I bring them; he knows me;
And smoke is our word.

And then I am silent.
But he the undoer—
Ah, the fierce laughings
Of flame to itself.

The eggshells, the cardboard—
Matter into spirit—
No wonder he adores me,
And comes there every day.

# OLD NAMELESS

Hephaestus, Vulcan, or perhaps
Old Nameless, dancer until dead,
Lie down awhile; or if you must,
Go jig and grin on graves instead;
Go slide on ice, go walk on water;
Any cool thing can be hotter.

Trample dew; go tread the sea,
Or, rage insisting, some man's house
So far from here I'll never know
By reek of paint or roasting mouse.
And yet I would not harm my brother.
Go melt one Pole, and then the other.

Be you busy, I care not
So it be elsewhere, master mine;
For you are that, as I could prove
By taper, torch, or turpentine.
Take my left hand, right hand, both;
But swear me then this little oath,

O, master flame: that you will spare
My books and papers; these two beds;
The dishes—do not sport with those,
Nor with the frames about the heads
Of certain young ones; nor the sill
That warmed her Wednesday, lying ill.

# SODDEN NOVEMBER

Sodden November
Is weeping for summer.
Or maybe not so.
The slime of leaves, the sleep of trees
Could be cold secret luxuries:
Sweet shivers of content
At riches spent.

Which were not wasted.
They are the liquid
Bed he desires.
Mountains of mist, and rivers of rain:
The heart of the world can rest again,
Under this grey profound
Of water and ground.

## LET ME LISTEN

I cannot thank you, rain, enough.
You would not hear me anyway.
You have your noises—let me listen
As the dark grass will all day.

I am not grass, I am not ground,
I do not live by water song;
Except as through this blessed glass
I feed on sound—may it be long—

Of drops that drive into the heart
And bring like blood the brightness back.
And yet not blood, and yet not mine
That cold deep world, crack under crack.

The fields of November
Fit like a lion's hide:
Old, dreaming lion,
Cold, sleepy ground.

The hollows and the rises,
The boulders, the long swells,
All of them are one there,
Breathing under brown.

But faint breath, and slow beat:
The fields of November
Fit like a warm skin
The dark of the world.

# DECEMBER SETTING

What death more wonderful
Than day's in winter?
All the cold west burns,
Burns to be near its insatiable lover,
The dark.

Cunning with hunger,
The two of them mingle
Their hectics—fiery,
Fiery the fusion, and smoky, of living
And lifeless.

Oh, the white heat of it,
Tempered to crimson:
And crimson—oh, lovers,
Oh, lovers of dying—to terrible black
Under black.

The quickest movement of the quickest bird
That comes in winter, then is gone again
(But comes again, finding our suet good;
Then off; then back; and now he wipes his bill)—

That quickest movement marks the flick of time
Mankind has been here (now he brings his mate:
Less gay, more greedy; and the two contest;
Not with each other; no, the stranger there)—

Has been in houses that the wildest dream
Of the first wing, before the world was cool,
Could never have imagined standing (six
More strangers: they descend; they have it all)—

Standing here this moment, this ticktock
Of cosy time; then gone again (Oh, God,
Oh, history. These little darting eyes:
Too old to read. Nor mind, mind to remember).

# ENEMY COLD

My enemy, cold,
Waits into the winter
To show me how cunning
He is, and serious.

Strange, I forget.
I think he has mellowed.
It takes him forever
To kill the good autumn.

But then he is done,
And here I am softer
Than Indian summer,
Than worm in the wainscot;

Here I am dead,
If once he can sting me.
So in by the boarding,
And thin over thresholds,

Crafty, he comes.
Then I double the doorglass;
Stuff the least crevice.
But he is not exiled.

Here he is now;
Is near; he must have me;
And may, some midnight
When I am grown listless.

## DECEMBER CATS

Less and less they walk the wild
Cold world of dark, of windy snow.
Curiosity comes in;
There is nothing more to know;
Examines corners; yawns and dies,
Warm under lamps and buzzing flies.

The oldest beast, with panther head,
The latest yielded: ran in tracks
Himself had punctured; hid by stones,
And pounced, and crackled mice's backs.
But now that all midwinter wests,
Even he the ranger rests.

# DOUBLE GOOD

If I can wonder what this animal thinks,
Sitting and watching or not watching me,
Does he do likewise? That is what I wonder.
Is something in him free as I am free?

Free, I mean, to seek what is not given,
And to despise all else? For if I knew,
And he knew, and the strangeness were destroyed,
What dreadful silence then between us two.

For now we talk; absurdly, we do talk,
And neither understands more than he should.
If all, we were as one; but now in dark
We keep distinction, which is double good.

No more than with another man I know,
No more than with a second beast he sees,
Past the fine twilight of this interval,
What each one is forever, if God please.

# WINTER HOUSECLEANING

Thursday

Tomorrow to the white pine
Patch where in November,
Solitary, I whacked off
Dead limbs, and left them.

Snow tonight, and no wind.
Well, if nothing changes,
Kerosene and old tires
Will smoke in every opening:

Will crackle as I drag there,
Thorny, a poor thousand
Pieces of the deep grove
That are at last but litter.

Once they were soft green.
Then the end of sunlight.
After that, a grey maze.
Tomorrow, woods to walk in.


Saturday

Not tomorrow—oh, no.
Yesterday I started:
Stumbled to the bonfire
With long ones, with short ones;

But still it is a wild place,
And I am not its tamer.
Oh, no. Time is.
(Sir, take it easy.)

Sunday

And yet they are a great thing:
Clean aisles to stroll in.
Possibly my strong sons—
Christmas, I'll ask them.

# LICHEN

Boulder in the meadow, world in the world,
And lichen upon it: field in a field.
On the smooth top there, death's grey grain
Creeping by centuries, circular, small:
Whosoever watches, still but a stain
Spreading in one place, waiting to be all.

Oh, the cold time yet, oh, the slow years
Till granite is covered, and sleep overpowers.
All the great rock there, grim as the world,
Whitened with death's wheat, motionless, mute:
Whatsoever wind, no leaf uncurled;
Whatsoever rain, no sweet green shoot.

Not that it hates this, tightening hold
On the hair of the stone, on the scalp of the world.
Ready for ice cap, ready under drought,
Ready now for nothing or for all, it lies,
Putting invisibly its feelers out
For the last great changes. Lichen is wise.

# WILD PANSY

Delphinium, haunt of hummingbirds,
White phlox, at sunset whiter still,
Stonecrop, corpse-cold, and feverfew
That seems a daisy yet is not,

You sleep more deep than Johnny-jump-up,
Who in cold spring, impertinent,
Will stare each early riser down,
Then call that windy world his own.

And so it will be. Such an eye
Dreams nowhere else in wintry earth.
I think it opens even now.
Cat nap for him is death enough.

# EPIGRAMS

## ART IS JUST

Art is short and art is long.
Work done this morning waits on time.
But time waits too. The oldest song
Still burns in eternity's quicklime.

And may be diamond there or dust.
Time cannot tell. Yet it was known
From the first blazing. Art is just,
And broods in eternity's brimstone.


## COMEDY

The world will not be understood.
Put on a sword, put on a hood.
Listen. Can you hear me? Good.
The world will not be understood.


## TRAGEDY

The world is something I must try,
However hard, however high.
Though I stumble, though I die,
The world is something I must try.

## FREEDOM

To be what no one ever was,
To be what everyone has been:
Freedom is the mean of those
Extremes that fence all effort in.

## HUMILITY

Let all men be what they would be?
I will. But let them tell me too
The utmost they expect of me,
That I the more may pleasure you.

## ATLANTIC

The ship's prow,
Great horse's head above unseen great hooves and knees,
Unflinching, through the bitterest green seas
Bites now;
And now;
And now.

## TOURIST

I passed Olympus in the night,
But had I passed by day
I still could tell you less of it
Than blind Homer may.

## GOOD AND EVIL

There is no man alive loves evil; none
Knows how to do so even if he would.
And this is strange; yet stranger, what each one
Hugs to himself as better than the good.


## PESSIMIST

Happy the man whose every dawn
Is last, and yet tomorrow shines.
What splendor, though it be the meanest
Morning. And tonight he dines.


## INCONSISTENT

Let no man see my girl;
Let all see, and admire.
Why do I contradict
Myself? Do not inquire.


## CONGENITAL

Beauty and strength were born in you, my soul,
Or else are missing; nor will come by thrift.
You may not add a part unto the whole:
The effortless, original free gift.

## RELATIVE

As time goes, and lives last,
   One winter is not long.
Except to starving mice: then vast
   Eternities of wrong.


## SUSPENSE

Get out, come in. Where have you been?
I know. Things do. So you are late.
Kiss me. Lie here. I tell you, dear,
I hardly could both breathe and wait.


## SONS

Riches would be well;
And happy work, and praise.
But most, may they keep liking
Each other all of their days.


## COLD BEAUTY

Woods, flaming in winter sunset,
Had best be witnessed warm indoors.
There is no heat in all that hectic;
Nor—wait, child—from Orion's stars.

## MARTIN HOUSE UNVISITED

Sixteen rooms, and none too narrow;
All of them high, for wind and view;
But random wren or sweet tree swallow
Is so far all that fate will do.


## GRAVITY

Snow is so light, how can it fall?
She was so sweet, how could she die?
I cannot tell you, child; but all
Things do love earth; yes, even the sky.


## WARNING

God will be hard to love.
Nature does not assist.
She was the jealous one
When daylight and chaos kissed.


## FRANKNESS IN FRIENDS

Frankness in friends must never be:
No words to set each other wise.
It was by love they learned to see,
Not by deliberate sunrise.

## KNOWLEDGE ENOUGH

The final freedom I desire:
To know what Homer, Shakespeare, knew;
And tough Cervantes: don and squire—
Halfway between them, that will do.


## GOOD APPETITE

Of breakfast, then of walking to the pond;
Of wind, work, rain, and sleep I never tire.
God of monotony, may you be fond
Of me and these forever, and wood fire.


## LAST HOUSECLEANING

Empty, my mind, of web and dust;
Of diamond too, and sharpened gold;
Of everything, and if you must,
Of my own self, grown old and cold.